THE SEEDS HAVE BEEN SOWN

with love…….

ANNA

ISBN 13   978-0692606582
ISBN 10   0692606580

DEDICATION

This book is dedicated to our great God who
makes all things possible

A Prayer

Oh Lord please help all who have lost their way find You. You are always forgiving and waiting with open arms, so please let them discover Your love and mercy. Open minds to understand that it is never too late on this earth to choose You. Please let those on the wrong path desire to enrich their hearts and belong to only You. Dear Lord please forgive us all for our sins.

Amen

PREFACE

As He walked the earth, Christ wondered if there would be any people who had faith when He returned.

The world is changing so rapidly that spiritual lives are being ignored while physical lives are demanding whatever they want whenever they want with little thought of morality. Where are all of the Christians; especially the Catholics?

Deep inside of us there is a place where we can go to truly look at ourselves if we choose to. It is a place where we push all of the values, thoughts, and behaviors that we do not want to acknowledge about ourselves.

This storage place can be brutally honest, and so it is very seldom visited by most people because the things seen are very startling. The few times that we do go there, very rarely do we automatically accept what we encounter.

Most of us consider our ways appropriate to what we are doing or the age that we live in. Concentration is on our daily tasks and earthly wants, and so we do what we feel we need to in order to obtain the outcomes that we desire. This thinking appears to be rational at the time and believed followed for necessity.

When we think of eternity, we think of it as a very distant occurrence, and most of the time we do not include our "forever" in the decisions that we make. Somehow everything will work out, and our eternity will be what we want it to be even if we sin to obtain the outcomes we want in this world.

The one thing that is generally ignored and left out is our soul and taking care of the spiritual part of our lives. We combine the physical with the spiritual, and we live by the physical. Little thought is given to the importance of the soul and how the condition of the spirit makes us happy or sad, content or displeased, or irritated or calm.

We look around at others and think that we must fit in with what others think is normal and acceptable. Even if we disagree, we often say nothing so that others will not think we are different or odd. We must fit in we think, so we will suppress our beliefs to this end.

As we grow, we do not even notice that our spiritual life is ignored until it is not even a thought. Even if we attend Church or believe in God, much of the time the here and now takes precedence over beliefs.

More and more most live for this world and stop noticing until finally we completely disregard our God's laws and ways. We only see the way we need to live life so that we can strive to gain what we want on this earth. We become so oblivious to who we really are that no matter what is pointed out to us we cannot see our true selves. As they say, many have eyes but do not see, and many have ears but do not hear.

Life becomes this world only, and the spiritual world is never noticed even though we pass it by moment after moment. We pass by the love that is so great and given so freely, and we are so full of pride we truly believe we know all. This way of existing leads to insensibility, and then we not only harm ourselves but we harm those around us. Whether by action or word, we hurt those we love and those who believe we understand what we are doing because they trust and follow.

The way that we make our choices and how we decide what we will feed in our lives will determine whether we consider the spiritual life we own. We all have free will to choose, and the choices we make will control who we are. Money, status, or material things do not make us who we are. It is the morals, beliefs, and rules we choose to live by that will determine who we are.

Yes, we will make mistakes and look back with some type of regret. But again, we make the choice on whether we will continue to live making regrets or begin to make memorable moments that can be looked back on with a warm heart.

Eternity is waiting for each one of us. How many days we will live on this earth are numbered, and we do not know that number. When the day the angel of death finally visits us, it is up to only us whether we will be ready for our judgement or not. For those who do not care about eternity, the devil waits patiently to apply the horror that he has planned. For those who believe in God and want to spend eternity with Him, they have a given timeframe that only He knows. This is the time given to become worthy to spend eternity in His presence.

He came to the world and gave His very life to save each of us. The agony and torture He experienced was more than worth it to Him because He loves each of us so.

He has given us a free will to use to serve Him or ourselves. He has given each of us a seed to grow, and we must feed that seed or let it go.

LOOKING
BACK, I SEE

I sit and look out of my window
My life is near its end and I look up to Heaven
That my end is near I know that I must reap what I did sow
I glance back over the years that I was given

What I see as I look back is great and constant love
When confused and from the narrow path I would wander
Help would always come to my aid from Above
Ignoring the grace, down the wide path I went and did not ponder

I have always believed that God does exist
Although action has not always been taken to serve Him
And the reality that He is always in our midst
Had many times in the past been considered a silly whim

As a child I was taught a simple prayer to say at night
And before I would slip into bed I would on my knees recite
Then I would lie down and look at the stars so very bright
Not remembering God as the thought of Him took flight

I was fortunate as I chose eventually to grow in belief of the Unseen
But many people who I have known have never believed
Not as a child and certainly not as a teen
Continuing to grow they never their God received

Though a believer sin I constantly did do
Even though my conscience continued to rebuke
And the acts I was committing I should not do I knew
I never asked why or tried with the devil to dispute

So many mistakes in my life I have made
And I used my will as I pleased my way
Not considering His laws as to me they bade
Not even contemplating that each one could be my very last day

Oh the years that I did ignore my Lord
My life was mine and I had to live it you see
I attended Mass while fidgeting and acting bored
And the time went slowly as I knew inside I must be free

But what does free really mean
Did my life ever really allow me liberty
Was the happiness great or very, very lean
Or through all my days did I only flee

As I moved through the time given
I knew that I had always loved Him
That so very deep inside to Him I was driven
Even though at the time the feeling was shallow and dim

The days I have lived I mostly thought of me
I did not mean to be selfish but who else would know my needs
To confession I did not go as I did not believe in the keys
And I always forgot about the One who for all did truly bleed

Slowly I began to perceive things differently
It took many years to change what I really did see
But over a long span of time my opinion did change gradually
And what I started to realize was the life that was meant to be

I understood that to each is given a length of time to stay
A time to use the gifts that were received
A time to comprehend and live each day
It is this time that must be used to serve and Heaven to achieve

It is up to everyone to grow each day progressing every way
And this must always be done and each must believe
There is no time to feel but thankful every sweet day
And to lean on Him and always to Him cleave

I thought of the blind classical tenor who slowed his pace
And sang with heart and soul to the Great Throne
He offered his gifts with a smiling face
His grand attitude and thought all should hone

The talent that was given to the singer
Was used to soothe those listening to the music
He sang like the angels and people did linger
Listening to the beautiful meaning of the lyric

Such an impressive gift was given with great love
A love offered freely to each person individually
Each person is watched and loved from Above
Each person is called by name and their needs considered fully

That was what our Lord told all many times to do
To love their neighbor purely as they love themselves
To pray for others as they kneel humbly in the pew
Seven Commandments ask all to love others as did the twelve

Knowing this but not quite understanding I proceeded on
Trying to put others first before the desires I perceived
A happy face I would always try to don
A plan to help others I would try to conceive

But oh as my usual ways drove me to behave
I could justify and know that my recipient was not worthy
So the help that I would give someone I would save
And by this method kept my ways and stayed within me

No comfort came deep inside me by these actions
So different routes I tried to take for silent and constant relief
No material thing, human, or pastime could stop the dissension
Everything that I tried would not prevent continuous grief

Why, I thought, does life bring such sorrow
When a good life in the person's opinion they try
And thought is given to what will be accomplished tomorrow
Yet the soul still languishes and each day the spirit cries

But again the spirit within did give an enormous sigh
When will perception finally sink deep inside
When will it be realized that joy and happiness I cannot buy
That living each day my way will not the final fate hide

I recognized I would always live a life of disquietude
Unless I learned to faithfully listen for and hear His voice
Knowing His sweet tone would give me certitude
I knew His voice would be the only one to make me truly rejoice

Suddenly I realized that the world I live in offers consolation
A way for my life to exist is part of His laws
These laws offer joy and happiness not deprivation
I must try to banish and rid myself of my flaws

I must remember that vile voices will always be heard too
Listening to them will lead me away from peacefulness
The wicked voices I must constantly see through
As sinful suggestions they will always make to bring sadness

The way ahead must be used carefully to choose the right ally
Not to prefer the wicked one who will always say anything
Hoping to lead me to his despicable ways and awry
It is time to look about life and see what now it brings

Most, I know, trust that they can do all their life as they please
And believe as time goes on the pendulum will not swing
That they do not need to fight for what is right and holiness seize
No need to live life by the Commandments and serve the King

The story of the friar is an important one to tell
In the field he was placed with his Guide beside him
And on each side, one edge from Heaven and one edge from hell
Frightened he looked at his holy Guide with a face that was grim

He was told plainly that the fight he must dare
And all of his resistance was entirely in vain
But he was not to fear as his Guide would be there
And together they conquered the evil and wicked that came[1]

I know that I must fight the same fight too
And the way through life should have very close attention
Remembering that judgment will come on everything I knew
So the end fate will truly be my very own invention

I think of all of those I have known through the years
People living by what they feel and want whether old or new
Some have hearts full of love and others live lives full of tears
Examining what is inside all must eventually do

God allows them by free will to choose their path
As from the garden they can select Heaven for their ban
They can choose to ignore His laws and face His wrath
And disregard that He took clay and did mold man

Or they can with their free will choose the great God and obey
And live with Him in Heaven as new Adam bought
So all must decide wisely and use history to help along the way
Looking to see how all those before did in their life wrought

Those who read were told of different ends after adieu
The medieval teacher described and advised outcomes
The good or bad consequences he outlined and drew
He knew an account of their lives was looming to see the sum

I looked at Heaven again and thought of the way after death
No sound is heard or sight seen of a soul floating away
The body is put out of view and does not take another breath
How can one leave so quickly and without a final say

I wonder how many spirits leave this earth each day
But life on this planet goes on and humans continue to play
No matter if the sun is shining or the sky blue or grey
Only a few indeed will stop and to God pray

Now I understand that I have been dividing my existence
I live in the world and think of this world as I go through time
Then in quiet moments I think about God and His great essence
But never the two do I combine so that I can persistently climb

While I live earthly life I act only from my selfish will
At Mass I think of God and my will rests as I pray
Then as I leave the Church I return to my will to satisfy and fill
And this is why I claim to be Christian but always forget the way

The realm about me is bursting with spiritual beings
But my time is filled with material things and prosperity
The spiritual world that surrounds me is fleeting
I live a divided life and cannot see the religious world with clarity

Our Lord told us very plainly what types of hearts there are
There are hearts that never in God believe
Hearts that only from God flee and hearts only earthly things jar
And those who give their hearts and with God interweave

Hearts of humans behave one way or the other
They either stay consistent or through the stages ascend
And at what stage they do stop depends on them not on another
The ideal destination will be found by having God as a best friend

What stage of life am I truly in and where am I today
Is there time to change and heal before the final call
Will He say I have been found wanting and only come halfway
And as the Lord looks down will in the sand He scrawl

I know that I must be judged like every other one
My God's beautiful countenance I will see
I will look into a face that is brighter than the sun
The time is coming and will not be belated for me

What will happen at that moment in time
Will I fall to my knees and beg Him for forgiveness
Will He allow me to Heaven with Him climb
Or throw me into darkness as Satan stands as witness

Again I think of the many people I have known throughout this life
Some have been kind and others not so caring
Many liked to be friendly and just as many liked strife
Various ones had few morals while others hardly erring

Now I think of them as receivers of the seeds
How do they now choose to live using the Word conveyed
What deeds are they selecting and is there fertile ground or weeds
Is it to God they look or to worldly things their lives do fade

The Sower of the seeds gave the kernels with love
What they do with what they were given is up to them alone
They must look deep inside and pray for guidance from Above
For everyone they meet they impact with their very tone

I look into the seeds that have been sown.........

To each who has heard the Great Word but turns the heart away, beware of the precipice on which you stand

THE SEEDS
THAT FELL
ON THE PATH

The Sower of the seeds spread the seeds arbitrarily
Some seeds fell on the path and the devil gathered them up hastily
These seeds did not land on fertile soil and were found easily
There was no interest by the hearer so they will live aimlessly

....

Ah but remember very carefully this
Those who do not bow to God then to Satan they do bend
Bowing to the devil he will take those to the abyss
They choose to ignore God so they choose hell for eternity to spend

After much thought about those who refuse to believe in God
The sad conclusion that has been arrived at ultimately
Is that those who are nonbelievers only through life plod
And the grace and love offered are disregarded subsequently

What is found to be so troubling when they doubt the Divinity
Are all of the things disbelief causes the multitudes to miss
If one listens, doubters say that none should trust in the Trinity
In the cynics' lives they have totally missed God and sight of Bliss

By disregarding and ignoring the Heavenly Maker
They miss the great Inventor and put man as the supreme being
And believing they are the ultimate they often become takers
All of earth is for them to ravish as their thinking is not foreseeing

Beautiful graces are not perceived and they sport silly whims
They refuse to look around them and see the awesome miracle
Do they think nature just occurred and did not come from Him
Has man ever made such splendor without first the original

That all seen just happened randomly and nothing was planned
Trees produce and give oxygen just so man can breathe
And man was given legs so that he can walk and stand
The human form protected as the entire body with skin is sheathed

Look around and see how different ecosystems thrive
Each built with a multitude of complementary living creatures
Some above the water flourish and some underneath dive
All with different contributions and specially made features

Someone very carefully planned out all that they do see
And made a world that rejuvenates itself by replenishing its needs
From the largest mountains to the very small and important bee
Continuing to change as needed and evolving as it proceeds

These wonders are all overlooked and man tries to take control
Of a world not understood but a world to be ruined as pleased
Only visible things are sought and wanted by body and soul
Missing the spiritual world until their essence the devil has seized

They also overlook the faith gained from the beautiful Scripture
A wonderful history missed that was laid out telling what occurred
A past told down through ages giving a stunning picture
And a history that by some have been completely unheard

Without Scripture they have no depth to contemplate
How a new covenant began between God and man
And started with the Sacrificial Lamb to totally compensate
A covenant that will last the rest of history's span

No knowledge is believed necessary and there is no need to learn
The way to eternal life and a brand new earthly way to live
How the Savior died for all and how His heart does yearn
And all that He has always done and all that He did give

By shunning faith in God they have nothing that lasts
They have nothing to believe in except for things that disappear
Their lives go by with only a vanishing worldly cast
Eventually all is gone and they look around with astounding fear

They continue on and miss the hope of soothingly being forgiven
A blessing lost that can turn to despair and eventually to madness
Those who do what are considered terrible things are driven
To live with the memory and throughout life tortured by sadness

Those who believe remember the apostle Judas
Judas decided to follow the devil and turn Jesus in
He betrayed his God as Caesar was betrayed by Brutus
Judas went into total despair and felt nothing but chagrin

Judas gave the silver coins back but he was lost in the dark
He knew he had forsaken his Lord and let the evil one in
He believed God had turned His back and his eternity was stark
He hung himself as he did not believe in absolution for his sin

So those who do not believe miss the comfort of God's blessing
And they hold on to their past and remorsefully live out their days
Continuing to hurt others and the results of their acts guessing
Afraid to face the unknown while holding fear in their soul ablaze

They clutch that fear refusing to go to Mass missing the great gist
Declining to walk over the threshold and into the Holy Home
Where love lingers and offers the touch of being gently kissed
Ignoring spirits of angels and Saints present from floor to dome

The Place where all can visit and state their many needs
And see the spectacular Mass where Heaven truly meets earth
Where those who believe pray together and recite the Creed
And thank a merciful God above for the notice of their worth

The imagination wanders and although it cannot be heard
Christians know that the angels sing and surely their voices raise
The songs sung with adoration are through love transferred
And Holy, Holy, Holy is vocalized in thanksgiving and praise

When the priest raises his hands with the bread and wine
The Holy Spirit descends and all there realize
That turning the bread and wine to body and blood is not a sign
But through the Holy Spirit the changes really do materialize

All of the statues and mosaics are pictures for all to see
Figures of the Lord and those important to Him as well
Depictions of Heavenly beings and events that set Christians free
Illustrations to help all recall the Passion do they tell

Those missing this exciting communion with God above
Continue on their way with no touch or warm relief
They understand nothing of the Great Sacrifice given in love
Nonbelievers miss out and through life their hearts aura is grief

They miss the great Eucharist the body and blood of the Lord
The Heavenly food required to enter into eternal Splendor
The bread and wine turned by Heaven as a loving reward
The food and drink given for all from the One so kind and tender

At the Last Supper Jesus gave those at table the bread
He said "This is My body which will be given up for you"
Then He took the wine and holding the cup said
"This is the cup of My blood, the blood of the covenant so new"

Remember in John's Gospel Jesus said to those
"He who eats my flesh and drinks my blood has eternal life"
The words from the King not just words that John did compose
For those who refuse, Bliss is lost and eternity will be full of strife

Those who persist in disbelief miss this great sharing
They do not understand the loving deed done to provide this gift
The atheists go through life ignoring the Sacrifice and uncaring
Not noticing the huge rift or how far from Paradise they drift

Along with Mass they miss the Holy Orders who offer all aid
Those who serve God with body and soul each and every day
Those who spend entire lives praying with hope that does not fade
Who are always there to help anyone find again their way

The Holy Orders are a Sacrament and work to administer the rest
The head of these holy servants is the successor of Peter
The Pope, the head of the Church, and the current one very blest
To the poor, the helpless, and the lowly he is defender and greeter

The Lord started the Catholic Church and gave to Peter the keys
For centuries Catholics have read this in the saving Word
The Church that stands strong and is there for everyone who sees
But those who refuse to read and believe think this all absurd

Those who choose to ignore miss the holy servants' helping hands
And they miss the opportunity for listening ears and prayers
They walk past those waiting for them and into a lonely land
Ignoring the aid that would help them become Heavenly heirs

The chance to encounter all Sacraments is missed and ignored
The Rites given freely offer soothing faith, hope, and love
Instead of learning about the Sacraments they hastily get bored
They think the Rites silly and believe nothing is Above

The Sacraments present the pathway to a fulfilled existence
And believing that the Rites hold great power and provide peace
Leads to lives that have great joy and much less Holy resistance
The Sacraments offer to all who trust lifelong release

Baptism opens the door to spiritual life which offers Divine sharing
Confirmation offers a deeper faith and opens hearts for others
Marriage between a man and woman is blessed and increases caring
The holy oil is used to anoint the sick and add comfort for another

So all seven Sacraments are missed by those who choose to ignore
The gifts given by God to make earthly existence loving and bold
The acts that can change and enlighten down to the very core
The blessings that keep the heart warm and far from turning cold

They also miss the privilege of enjoying the Church's family
Where love and kindness prevail and all are invited to believe
Together with the Saints and angels all at Mass listen to the homily
And when all are not present they with Heaven grieve

The doubter overlooks a vast community of supporters
People who are there to help and work for all of those in need
A community helping to procure food, clothing and living quarters
Advocates who help those in spiritual distress so they will heed

The Church bands together to extend help to all worldwide
The caring that is offered is for everyone and ethnically blind
Any ridicule, prejudice, or even Christian death is taken in stride
And the support continues while the mindset is to help and be kind

So those who do not believe miss a fantastic family assembly
They struggle daily with only what they know and perceive
As they miss out on love and those who serve humbly
They never understand why in their lives they never fully achieve

They miss any opportunity to hope for the future
All they see is what is currently available they can feel and touch
They refuse to see what can be the continuous path towards torture
Instead of letting go of their normal they use it as a crutch

Doubters fail to realize and miss the graces offered freely to them
Not believing, they ignore opportunities to grow and be changed
And with graces unused the unbelievers on life blame the problem
They never grasp full meaning no matter how life is arranged

Mercy is given often to help them along their way
Yet they do not believe kindnesses are there to be enjoyed
God will not shout or send an angel with the grace to say
But He will persist until the unbeliever is thrown into the void

Still they insist on putting off God's graces with taunting
Finally He will say they have been weighed and measured
And that they have been found unacceptably wanting
Once that is announced they will no longer be treasured

They miss eternal hope and there is nothing to look for after death
How can a life be full of joy if there is nothing to look forward to
Do those who do not believe look forward to their last breath
How can they live their lives without feeling alone and blue

Hope cannot be just for the things wanted on this planet
Very few realize all that they desire in human form
This world cannot offer happiness forever for those who inhabit
They must ask God to be their Savior and they really must conform

For hope should be concentrating on the spiritual nature
Looking for eternal hope in what is wanted here and now is futile
Material objects, money, and status cannot offer what does nurture
Without expectation for the hereafter earthly life will be only brutal

So they are on the verge of missing an eternity so grand
A future so comforting that has been offered again and again
They insist to continue ignoring and sticking their head in the sand
And staying their course until the judgement has finally come then

They will miss a wonderful eternity where forever will be Bliss
Persisting to disregard forever and that they will one day pass away
Will lead them to the serpent who they will see and hear his hiss
Then it will be too late to ask for pardon and live forever His way

Living with Him in a cozy place where the sun always shines
And God is visible to make their hearts glad forever
Where all are loved and free for Heaven never confines
And the evil one is gone and will be seen again never

Where angels sing the most beautiful songs
And all are relaxed and feel at home and protected
A place where never again will be brought up all the wrongs
And all who are there are with each other interconnected

Remember Samuel when he was called
Samuel did not know God then or answer Him right away
He went to Eli three times and each time out of bed he crawled
Then Eli told Samuel to wait until God one more time did say

For God speaks once or twice or many times to man
Samuel chose God but they do not follow and do not comprehend
They ignore God's call and follow others' wishes and plan
And choose to turn away and to God offend

Sadly the love of their life is missed as God is thought impossible
Family and friends exist here but no love matches the Creator's
Yet all of this is unnoticed because there is no belief in the Gospels
They believe in themselves and consider this something greater

The love that is missed is given freely and is complete
It is for all and the souls are watched carefully
The care is for their needs and is attentive and discreet
All that is accomplished for them is done so very gracefully

The unbelievers miss the most fabulous friendship that exists
A God who takes time to talk to them even when they do not reply
A God who is there to hold their hand even when they resist
A God who never stops trying as He waits with a Heavenly sigh

The friendship that is offered never on this earth wavers
No matter who they may be or what they have done
God stays faithful until their end and offers His favors
What type of friendship on this earth matches this one

But those who currently do not believe are not alone
There is always someone near them even if unseen
They are invited by the Creator to become His very own
This offer they must choose to take before their soul is gleaned

They must ask the good Lord to return the seed
And then look deep inside themselves to see the soil there
The Lord will understand and give them what they need
Then they must stay with God through loving Him and prayer

From that point forward they must continuously grow their seed
And thank God daily for all that He has shown them
Only then will they stop their incredulous lives and finally be freed
And slowly over time they will turn into a treasured Heavenly gem

THE SEEDS THAT
FELL ON
ROCKY SOIL

The Sower scattered the seeds in the wind
Some seeds fell on stony ground and grew up quickly
The soil was not deep causing the roots to be thinned
When the sun began to shine the growth withered away swiftly

....

Instead of just giving laws He writes His love on hearts
He does this so all from the beginning will be on the right path set
This affection is given to everyone and is given from the start
But the seeds that fall on rocky ground are not ready for Him yet

When the Word is heard oftentimes they receive it with elation
But when any type of persecution comes because of the Word
The hearts with rocky soil abandon and change their fixation
Allowing the evil one to ensure that the initial passion is blurred

The great joy they feel they allow to dissipate hastily
Hearing different opinions they let the pressure sway
Others gripping evil ways are permitted to influence mistakenly
Still others separated from God lead them to betray

What a shame that those who find God so happily
Should leave so quickly to follow those who surround
To practice ways that lead their lives unnaturally
To walk away from a way of life that is so very profound

Fear or insecurity can skew thoughts and actions
And letting others influence too much will cause dissatisfaction
Many roaming in this world purposely cause distractions
So those who leave God follow sinful ways as a sad reaction

Fear and self doubt are debilitating emotions that can destroy belief
Letting others reign over feelings throws the follower into disarray
The wicked on earth take advantage and take power as a thief
Using this control to grab and hold its victim until the final weigh

Those with shallow roots allow others to lead them from God
The soil they have built in their heart is troubled and not lush
So others talk them away from Christianity and constantly prod
And the seed with the weak root they allow others to crush

What hold do humans and masked evil have and use on them
What important matters could pull them so far away
Are the ideas and wants of others who can hurt and condemn
Worth consideration when ultimately they will cause decay

What type of pressure or anxiety draws them to follow
What compels them to go by any whim of the time
Can they not think for themselves and are their lives so very hollow
Shadowing others and whatever is popular in the particular clime

The greedy coerce by claiming justice while taking others away
People petition for the rights wanted even if society they will harm
Thus confusing those with shallow roots by leading them astray
Inspiring psychological deterioration and comprehending alarm

These actions taken are for selfish reasons and no matter the cost
The burden should be on humanity as a few must be appeased
Courts waver under the demands that in front of them are tossed
As the few must realize victory and have their imagination eased

Those with rocky soil become angry and turn from God their face
What will those claiming justice say if they God's laws support
Of course each demand that comes along certainly has a case
So they must soothe for the claims letting others His laws distort

They disregard the actual issue but focus on the ones who demand
No thought is given to God but to the ways wanted by others now
They are angry about being in this state supporting the others' stand
In other words they pass by their God and to earthly humans bow

When anger is used for a claimed righteous earthly intention
And those who judge for evil causes do push away true morality
They only cause disservice and defend the evil dissention
Ignoring truth and goodness and seizing an unrighteous reality

This can lead to others pulling them from the Church
People detailing how Catholics are not a just community
Those with rocky soil listen to the news and perform no research
Believing that all Catholics are in a state of disunity

When evil is found in the Church and the public is surprised
The thought that it is the individual's fault is not considered true
And the entire Church and its ways are suddenly despised
As those who criticize or condemn think that all Catholics knew

Each individual is accountable and must answer for any sinful act
There are those throughout each part of society that cause hurt
That does not make each part of society evil and goodness lack
So a few disreputable cannot the entire Church subvert

Some within the Church took advantage and the Church has paid
What of other institutions and organizations that mistakes have made
Have they been so criticized or given the same grade
They forget that the Catholic Church the acts always have forbade

The Church obeys God's laws and some become upset at that
Those who follow others want to make their lives so very quaint
They point out faults of individuals and try the Church to combat
Though a few have caused unrest the Church still has her Saints

Their weak actions persist with gluttony and not taking time for Him
The electronic world has captured them and totally taken them in
Family and friends must be disregarded as the electronic whim
Has the shallow roots mesmerized and they ignore the domestic din

They forsake their Heavenly Maker to concentrate on silly things
And put their trust and hope on others' ads and constant posts
Believing all that is told to them whatever it may bring
Taking to heart all that is written as if the words were oaths

They turn their back on the finer things just to keep with the crowd
Overlooking all of the evil that goes on within the electronic cloud
While announcing all the happenings and forwarding so proud
And shouting to the invisible world excitedly and loud

All over the world some try wicked uses for this communication
No matter from conference room, apartment, or cell
The ease of lying and deception underpins the causation
Afraid not to be part, the seed they let die slowly saying farewell

Absorbed by things that do not save the soul but takes all their time
And disregarding God and who He has given to them to love
Will not offer them an avenue at the end to avoid the abyss or climb
Gluttony for earthly things will not aid in achieving Above

And those in this rushed world with time that goes far too quickly
Can become selfish practicing sloth with the time daily available
They turn aside completely ignoring the needy, elderly and sickly
Afraid if they do not follow the throng their lives will be unstable

Those who really need their time are pushed aside for later
Life on earth is to be lived and they must focus on peers and fads
It is not their fault others need help as that came from the Creator
So caring for those unable will make their lives frustrated and sad

Thinking time must be used for self and ignoring the needy to stray
Hurts everyone involved except the people who want their way
Those with thin tubers ignore the weak or aged keeping them at bay
And after all the smoke does clear their lives are spent and joy nay

Remember the parable about the barren fig tree
The owner of the fig tree told the gardener to cut it down
It had not produced fruit in three years and he wanted the land free
The gardener asked for time to fertilize and add dirt that was brown

"If it does not produce fruit I will cut it down for you next year"
This shows the Lord's patience and how He waits for them to bear
When they refuse to love Him and others He sheds a very sad tear
For they have let the foe pull them away and they no longer care

Trusting blindly can also lead them to believe all politicians' words
This can lead a country's people down a path of destruction
Some act as if they are afraid and dare not make their opinion heard
And act as if their vote is not important and not a necessary function

Those on stony ground do not know what to do
They follow heedlessly the lead of some put in trust of their nation
By ignoring politicians' strategy for a career that the officials hew
They permit some to dictate corrupt practices rotting the foundation

Approving any politician who ignores and pushes away their public
Creates a nation that includes tyrannical leaders who are corrupt
The greedy leaders act to take freedoms away from the republic
Persisting until rights and liberties are gone unnoticed and abrupt

Recall the rocky soil who allowed the religious leaders' hand
And with Roman politicians the leaders for their own power dealt
The sad soil agreed to have the Lord crucified with a brutal stand
While officials and leaders considered status not thorns and welts

Did those who cried "crucify" ask for mercy; where are they today
Are they worthy of the Paradise and gifts that God has made
Or are they deep in hell without daylight or any type of say
In distress forever and apart from God always as severed shades

And always there are those who believe they are of top station
Insisting with pride all below must bend and this acknowledge
Their lives and comfort come first no matter the frustration
So those below must see these needs and pay utmost homage

Instead of standing for moral justice and following the right way
The unfertile soil turns from God to please those who are a danger
Deceit and misrule abound while all involved must the game play
As the expectations are met of the powerful friend or stranger

Believing God does not really care they live by worldly mandate
Those they mimic hold the good life not found by following Him
The seed is almost expired and they have no desire for a clean slate
They do not yearn for pious justice and are fixed on the fiery brim

Do they not understand that the physical world offers nothing
It is only pride and money oriented and not concerned with souls
The devil works at luring all into this fold until His second coming
Satan tempts all who will listen in order to gain control

I notice some are very afraid of the laws of their Creator
So they run and hide allowing their roots to die from starvation
Turning to the world and deciding to be a Christian berater
And believing this world will keep them in a delightful situation

If God wants praise His laws must vary so their ways can exist
There are always exceptions seen that God must not have pondered
And it takes humans to determine how His decrees must twist
It is not they but Him who from the truth must have wandered

Look to Adam and Eve who lived in paradise so grand
Both were told of God's laws and all that He did demand
Not listening to their God they chose the evil one and to be banned
To a hard life in a plain and disarrayed land

It is possible those on stony ground are just anxious about God
Fearful that they will have to sacrifice and continuously mourn
And certain that those around them will see them only as odd
Those they will have to deal with will only see them with scorn

They become petrified to change their lives and gain delight and joy
Lives where material things and politics play little part in days
Ignoring those who try to abuse and use others as puppets and toys
Lives choosing mercy for everyone avoiding fog and cloudy haze

Anxious about living lives not filled with excuses or justifications
Or to take responsibility for actions and have a solid belief
Lives that build a notable world enjoying an array of moral relations
While inspiring friendship and joy not dissention and constant grief

They are nervous about pointing out the evil that exists
And they are not eager to begin praying that problems will be cured
Or to stop seeing God as the cause of evil Who fades in the mist
But linger in belief He does not do His job and evil must be endured

I see those around who are afraid to have faith in God who gives all
Frightened to be simple and sincere to the only One who counts
Deciding to turn from the One who to an amazing eternity can call
Certain that about their God faith they will denounce

Are they fearful prayers will not be met in their terms and times
And that God will choose to give something other than they asked
Or that He will never respond because of their moral crimes
Believing any love or goodness in their future will be masked

That there will never be comfort shown to them from Above
That God really does not know anything about them or their needs
And that He will not answer so they will never encounter the Dove
Believing there is nothing they can do about the unfertile seeds

Ah but remember the tax collector who was disliked by all
He wanted to see Jesus and climbed high into the trees
And Jesus knew right away that Zacchaeus was there to call
Jesus stayed with him that day and set one lost into one who sees

Those with dying seeds are afraid to hope for an eternity of Bliss
They turn and are unwilling to try to discover what is waiting there
Agreeable to accept what is offered in this world and the next miss
Then ready to die and be unable to climb the Heavenly stair

Can they not see through this world and what exists besides
That visible things are only a small part of what there really is
And unseen help is always nearby through caring Heavenly guides
Or that they are truly loved by what above is His

Do they not understand that eternity lasts forever
And what they choose on this earth after death will not change
That their decisions and the things in life they endeavor
Will bring them closer or to the great God estrange

Many feel uneasy taking true love and giving their love to another
The love that they have received freely and always unconditionally
That their earthly wants and cares He will only smother
And His goal is to take all and leave a life floundering miserably

Do they look at the ideals and thoughts that they have
At what they lust for as necessary and on this earth require
Reviewing worldly events that provide comfort and earthly salve
Actually judging loving Him will take all they humanly admire

Do they ponder the worldly things they wish to use or own
Or the actions that never really bring happiness or give joy inside
Acts that do not give love and spawn emotions that are only on loan
And the feelings that are false they partake in then they try to hide

They continue down a path being jealous of those they see
Begrudging others of what they want and who tell them what to do
Reasoning that God and His ways will never set them free
Thus the only thing that they can do is take to see them through

Their envy leads them to follow to make the right decisions
They tell themselves to use their will and disregard moral choices
While thinking daily living will give them appropriate visions
And all of their conclusions will bring happiness and rejoices

So those with rocky soil decide that faith is not needed
They have opted to ignore God and think like others and choose
That hearts are from their bodies made and not really seeded
The only ones that matter are others' philosophical views

Some believe money is the vital focus that they must seek
Wealth will cure all the problems that occur day after day
And the currency will certainly turn lives bright from being bleak
Being rich they know everyone will listen to what they have to say

The more money they can gain the happier they will be
Thinking of eternity is not necessary as they will buy integrity
Any morality that they need will be bought to impress the Trinity
Knowing when death approaches their forever will have dignity

Inappropriately their desire for riches increases beyond compare
And there is nothing that changes their focus from obtaining more
No matter how much they have they are not going to share
Finally money is the only thing they can find to adore

When they believe money is all there is and the rich are the highest
And trust all they do will make them visible to others or not
They look all around and accept those who are biased
And believe those who say Christianity is only a plot

The stony soil avoids persecution by not knowing God's ways
They refuse to pick up Scripture to help them understand
Ignoring Church they listen to others and walk around in a daze
Eluding criticism by deciding for God they will not take a stand

The time they must fear is when they feel they are the utmost
These thoughts make them like the devil when he chose to revolt
At that time Michael the Archangel looked around the cosmos
And said "Who is like God" and pushed Satan with a jolt

Satan walks this earth with a heart that hates
And those with stony ground are easy for him to take
Little is needed for the devil to gather them with different baits
Once their time is up in front of him they will quake

When the seed lands on a space not prepared
But joy springs up quickly and happiness is sensed
If the seed is not protected and no interest is declared
Then with no attempt to learn the new sensation is condensed

Many issues come up each hour and different interests gain
There is no time to go to Mass or even time to pray
And the times for giving attention and praise to God wane
There are things that must be done and time is needed to play

After work friends are met and a game is going to start
The weekends are for yard work and then a social time
Something is always started and it is too hard to part
So missing Church and singing songs cannot be a horrible crime

Priorities mount and continue to push God away
And even though He stands nearby they do not seem to care
It is very easy indeed to do as they please and stray
It is not long and finally there is no more time to share

That is when the devil knows he holds them in his hand
No more struggle is needed and they have made their choice
It is not that giving their will away was really ever planned
But they did not persist in trying or raising to God their voice

Finally lives consist of a variety of the seven deadly sins
None of the sins feel wrong as they practice them each morrow
Gradually without notice the amusement becomes quite thin
Then very soon the laughter dies and there is only sorrow

They no longer believe in one God but on earth many
Their focus turns to the moment only and what they desire
Inside they do not feel the need or want to oblige any
Their actions and feelings are only open to the highest buyer

How blind they become when they give their soul away
To a demon who could not care about them or to them give love
They continue on their path not realizing they forfeit their say
And slowly close the door that leads to the Lord above

Those whose seeds fall on unfertile and stony ground
Are given a wonderful gift to pamper and continue to grow
But the joy of the Word does not last and suddenly dies the sound
And they do not care to cultivate the seed the Lord did sow

God gives them free will to use to grow their seed
So they can use their free will to fertilize or for the seed to spurn
For those with rocky ground the free will is not used to feed
And Lucifer's demons ensure the roots will thoroughly burn

The free will is available throughout life on this earth
A change in attitude can start the seed to grow
To accomplish this Satan cannot be let in or given any worth
They must ask God back and in the fire the devil to throw

Recall the Israelites who in the desert roamed
They became impatient and with their free will chose
To build a golden calf from metals those nearby loaned
They laughed and danced until Moses from the mountain rose

The worshippers of the golden calf had caused great offense
And to those who danced for the calf chastisement they met
The way they chose to use their free will there was no defense
So those who turned from God without sorrow had to pay the debt

The laws given from Above were given with love
And following these rules will only give liberty
As the world's pressures fade away and objects are gotten rid of
Peace will enter in and come very soon inwardly

Just as those who went to the Sepulcher on the third day
Expected to see their Lord dead in the grave
Instead they heard the angel at the tomb say
"He is risen" and they knew that them He would save

Until that time they felt alone as well
They feared for their lives and waited to be taken
As their hope and belief in what Jesus said fell
He appeared to them and they knew they were not forsaken

Those with slight roots must decide if they will turn back to God
And live the good life without focusing on this world
They must choose before they die and are covered with earthly sod
And their soul is taken and to the underworld hurled

They do not know how long they have to live in this worldly state
The free will must be used to refuse and push away sin
This must be done before worldly existence ends so evil does abate
And before the end and the devil for eternity the souls win

They must think carefully about what their beliefs are
And take into account all that they have experienced
If they still insist on believing and living from God afar
Then for eternity the gap will be huge and they always distanced

For them it is not too late to fertilize and again begin to grow
They must start to put God and others first before themselves
Knowing then they will in the end reap bushels they did sow
They must read Scripture by taking their Bibles off the shelves

Remember Jonah who told God no and turned and walked away
He replied to the call with his free will and chose to tell God adieu
Jonah was put in the whale's belly for three days being dismayed
From that point on Jonah's will chose God's way and for God to do

So Jonah did as God said and went to Nineveh to give His message
Jonah was a prophet but he did not believe the people would heed
He was uneasy about the outcome and the impending presage
But the Ninevites took ashes and sackcloth atoning their unfed seed

Even though Jonah did not want to go and do as he was asked
He went and became angry when the Ninevites changed their ways
Jonah did not like the pardon showing from humans he was cast
And God showed how great He is by how rightly He did appraise

THE SEEDS THAT
FELL AMONG
THE THORNS

The Sower of the seeds scattered the seeds all around
Some seeds fell among spiny plants that did the seeds scorn
Many of these prickly plants grew up hastily from the ground
The seeds could not endure and were choked by the thorns

....

Often people hear the Word and they gladly accept
Then instead of deepening their understanding of the meaning
The message to the back of their mind is slowly swept
They have no sense of the evil that is constantly intervening

Faith in the Holy Trinity gives a lasting peace
They can accept faith seeing differently and seeing life anew
Or ignoring faith little change occurs and trying does finally cease
Suddenly they find themselves in a mist they cannot see through

They who once did gladly accept the mighty God's edicts
Over time have turned to living a divided existence
One minute they turn to God and then turn to the world's verdicts
Finally they choose to show complete Godly resistance

They need to look all around at what is happening today
The Church is being attacked from many different ways
Political bodies object to the Church's work leading people away
Those who want their immoral way are to God glad to disobey

What happened to the joy they formerly felt
When God they once did love and obey
Their belief continued on no matter what life dealt
Suddenly they turned their path to follow the worldly way

Have they not seen the mistakes they have actually made
They continue to strive towards things that will not please
Using God's name in vain and acting comparable to the sad shades
Waiting until it is too late to ask forgiveness even on their knees

There are many paths that they allow to lead them astray
Or many worldly fears that care not for them but pull them away
Ways that are attractive and might allow them today to play
But these are ways that will eventually make them sadly pay

The people whose seeds land among the thorns
Are those who used to believe in God and faithfully acknowledged
Now they turn to the world and with material things adorn
Choosing to dismiss their Savior and live on earthly knowledge

They may still attend Mass each weekend when they can
But Mass is missed if there are other plans that have been made
If Church is attended their phone messages they will need to scan
While gazing around to see who is there and how they are arrayed

There is no longing to listen and learn about their Master
No desire to hear the Gospels and grow their seed
They just keep thinking that the priest should talk faster
And they forget about the gift of how their Savior did bleed

The songs that are sung are not seen as praise to God
And too many verses only prolong the Mass
Their eyes grow heavy and they begin to nod
When it comes time to tithe they choose to ignore alas

Some always go to Mass but they ignore confession
They can ask God for forgiveness without intervention
No searching the heart is required or personal concession
There is also no need to consider future sin abstention

Remember the day that the Lord gave Peter the keys
He delegated the power to Peter to hold the keys of the kingdom
Whatever was bound on earth Heaven would also bind these
Whatever was loosed on earth Heaven would release them from

Thinking throughout life that confession is not necessary
Matthew should be read to see what the Bible says to all
The Scriptures are for every generation and are not temporary
It is important they realize and follow so they recognize the call

There are those who go to Mass because they are supposed to
They go because they were brought up to follow the status quo
Even though the earthly conclusions that they drew
Do not support the concepts that from the Mass flow

They ignore Scripture even if mortal sins have been committed
And still choose to take Communion the Great Sacrifice
This is of course just a routine learned and permitted
A way they have been taught to live and will certainly suffice

They disregard the grave consequences that will certainly come
And feeling very little requirement to ask forgiveness for their sins
They continue to participate in the Holy Sacrament and to succumb
A practice very hard to explain once eternity begins

And those who call themselves Christians but really do not adore
Grasp their worldly behavior and ignore the Church's preacher
They inspire others away from the faith considering religion a bore
Thus acting offensively to God disregarding the Holy Teacher

They must beware of offence to God and leading others astray
While at Mass pretending to be upstanding members of the Church
And when away talking and acting just the opposite way
Instilling doubt of the Church and causing ecclesiastical besmirch

They must also consider the way they instruct their children
Do they teach youth it is alright to disregard God's laws
That they should do as they please and be unpredictable then
Giving instruction to the young it is alright to support any cause

Some say that they believe in God and may even be charitable
But perhaps they run a business and focus on the profit
Always considering their wealth after expenses is inevitable
And knowing extra costs tacked on can be hidden for the audit

The attitude is that wealth must increase always without delay
There are many material objects wanted that cost a great deal
And they believe quality and quantity of physical goods convey
The importance of the owner and what in the world is real

If customers cannot be served because they cannot pay
Then the products or services are not really needed
Those customers can just do without and it will not bring dismay
Even if their health or living requirements go unheeded

The bottom line must be the disposal income made
If a little less service or product is given from what was promised
The bill will show the entire sum so it can be completely paid
They think the Lord will realize they are not being that dishonest

But remember those with money ample buying anything wanted
Can certainly not buy happiness, morals, or a wonderful eternity
So a life that yearns to earn more and more is daunted
And no matter how much is made there is no eternal certainty

Thus those thinking only of making money can turn miserable
Stress about losing their comfort and position can follow
No matter what is gained it is not enough and life turns invisible
They themselves choose in repetition to wallow

Think of the wealthy man whose harvest exceeded his sheds
He decided to build bigger barns to house his wealth
He would live securely for years drinking wine and eating bread
That very night death came upon him taking his good health

They must beware of storing up a great deal of acquired wealth
Needing more and more and sharing less and less
For death does not always announce itself and can come in stealth
So focus on wealth is futile when the final day cannot be guessed

Some who have seeds that fell among the thorns
Wish to live a political life and wish to run for office
Telling constituents they will work hard and voters will not mourn
They will ensure all supporters will not experience injustice

On the campaign trail many believe in God and religious morals
After being elected many frequently begin this to ignore
The belief is that they must protect their post and avoid quarrels
Trying to keep their position by not coming to the fore

To many religious freedom is no longer a law they will advocate
Whatever gets the representative ahead will be supported
The effort is on obtaining reelection and they must be delicate
If the laws get in the way they will have to be thwarted

Those who have a political life have a great deal to answer for
They oversee government that affects peoples' lives
They often decide if there will be local unrest or international war
Making their term productive or for confusion strive

Encouraging others to be dependent for food, housing, and support
In order to increase power and pretend fairness has been gained
Will in the end cause countless lives and peace will fall short
As those who are under the rule will feel degraded and chained

So to those who take public office and then to voters do not comply
And to those who believe they must connive to obtain their share
Contribute to the fall of their country and the global opinions eye
Then they will through judgement their sentence bear

The few taking action to participate fully as a public servant
And who work hard to create laws that make life better
Will have all the benefits realized by those who are observant
And for those of the country the release of their fetters

The media who skew the daily news fall into the same category
There are those with thorny soil grasping news blindly and believe
While many things told to them have a distorted story
And morals the media have are used for the news to conceive

Those things that are not on some media's agenda are downplayed
And the political ploy is to report what they want all to abide by
So those who believe without research listen and are swayed
And the believers do not hear the prejudice but only the battle cry

Much of the worldly news so shiny and bright of today
Hopes to lead those who believe to support the political path only
A path to lure the whole into a political order where all must obey
A world where the nation's populace will turn hopeless and lonely

Remember when Satan took the Lord to the pinnacle
And offered Him the whole world if He would to the devil kneel
Jesus was not fooled and knew He didn't need the physical
For He was willing to suffer so all could eternity seal

Then some with sharp soil disregard and rearrange the environment
They use ideas and technology to build empires or create exposure
And bionetworks are destroyed as a necessary requirement
The motivation is to make a life that is easy without disclosure

Water can be contaminated and make residents sick
Or crops may not grow and those working at the project are ailing
None of this matters as money must be made amply and quick
And justification of small paychecks reimburse the altered failing

No study is made of the long term effects for what is damaged
So how many species will be lost forever because of greed
Or how long will it take humanity to overcome what is ravaged
Yet God's design is cast off and the taker hears no one plead

And then there are those who use technology to hurt carelessly
The ones with choking thorns who choose to harm without thought
Often post in the electronic world anything they please recklessly
Not realizing how their actions upset and hurt others for naught

Is it so important to injure others to make their day
To make themselves feel important and great by belittling
Believing it is their right to give their opinion and have their say
Using such a sorry way to act and to promote unsettling

What do they gain by telling lies or creating an unimpressive story
Hurting others and to the public displaying bad judgment
These actions will never to themselves bring glory
It only allows those participating to be repugnant

And let them not forget that bearing false witness
Eventually only ruins the bearer's life not the one being discussed
Truth always comes out in the end and displays fitness
Those who are mean and false will lose respected trust

Remember the Commandment that Jesus gave His disciples
"You shall love your neighbor as yourself" is the second greatest
They can find Jesus' Commandment in the Gospels
And they should follow this law rather than against God attest

The Great One gave Ten Commandments for all to follow
The first three are about a living bond and loving God above
The next seven are about loving their neighbor and easing sorrow
All ten are given as a way to live life and truly love

God's laws stay steady and are guiding posts
They will not change because a human thinks they must
It does not matter the case presented or the current boasts
God's laws will continue to prevail until all men turn to dust

Many believe that the Commandments hold them back
That in order to be free and happy they must ignore
Living life within these confines will take their lives off track
And following God's laws will certainly not allow them to soar

They need to think hard about what the Commandments can do
The laws can free them from all that they have been addicted to
The guiding posts can change their insincere point of view
And the decrees can help them feel peaceful and no longer blue

Take a look at those who believe fornication is a good start
That God will just have to understand they are not yet ready
They must try out the arrangement before giving away their heart
Living like this can create a bad foundation making lives unsteady

It is too easy to walk away when a storm comes along
One may love and the other one just uses for their pleasure
Having someone new enter their life starts a new song
Then the one walked away from is no longer a treasure

How hard it is for some to let go when they have believed
That their lives together would only grow dearer
The one made no commitment and the other one cleaved
One left when they wished and the other cried as it became clearer

I know families on this earth can also be misused
These people can be taken for granted and often pushed aside
They are still part of life in this world even if excused
They are often seen as pests and each day love denied

Those who do not honor and find it very easy to simply justify
Believe those in their life do not need respect nor do they matter
The only emphasis is that the justifier's needs should be clarified
Their life has utmost value and they will not be pushed to latter

But one day a family member grows sick or experiences old age
Some incapacitated require care and patience on a constant basis
The younger family members feel as if they have been put in a cage
They cannot help the sick and old and they cry and plead their cases

Then unexpectedly the day comes and there is no one there to assist
The aged or sickly have gone and no more do they need aid
Those left behind are in shock and begin to cry and their hands twist
They now are very sorry and miss the one who did away fade

Most forget that God watches over and loves each and every one
He concentrates on the person not the worldly sum
He expects those with thorny soil to care for all and leave out none
To certainly care for each and every one until eternity comes

The Trinity does not take people as retribution
Each is given time to perform their part of the plan
The acts they perform in their part of the design are their solution
Choosing whether they act by God's laws or by the rules of man

The day that each will die was decided before birth
God does not punish by taking a person from this existence
The date is marked for this as the day they will leave this earth
The key is to care for those as long as necessary with no resistance

Lazarus laid at the rich man's door covered with sores
The rich man did not harm Lazarus he just ignored the poor man
Not even the scraps from his table did the rich man take outdoors
Lazarus died and was carried to Heaven as his eternity began

The rich man died as well and was sent to hell
He looked up and saw Lazarus in Abraham's embrace
He asked if Lazarus could alert his brothers who on earth did dwell
Abraham said the brothers would not listen and he denied the grace

As was told about those who have the world's goods
And see their brother in need yet close their hearts
How could God's love possibly abide in them or would
Those who do not think of others from God will always part

These same also overlook the gift of health they received
And they curse God about a blemish, a gray hair, or a pound
Instead of being thankful for well being they always look grieved
Through life instead of giving thanks they stare sadly at the ground

They certainly are not perfect as they hoped they would be
Their toes are all crooked and their teeth have a space
They need to get help as their imperfections they know all can see
And the thorns in their soil are signs they have not accepted grace

Suddenly they look around and they begin to see
The fabulous gifts given them and the miracles of health and grace
They see a child with a leg gone up to the very knee
And a young father goes by wrapped in a body length brace

Abruptly they understand how privileged they are and blest
How they have feet and legs and arms that they can always use
Then just as quickly they forget to thank God and humbly confess
But rush to call a friend and complain about a little bruise

Ignoring grace continues and those who are choked by thorns agree
With atheists that traces of God must be taken out of the public eye
They agree the statues and religious items the public should not see
They insist religion be removed from the civic with a loud outcry

Most of the time these people are only a handful who rage
But just a few can go through the system and achieve their goal
Many want God available to their families on the public stage
But those who are offended by God bear their Godless soul

Why should those who truly believe have to do without
And those with disbelief get their way with a shout
Do all have to suffer and go through this ridiculous bout
Christians will continue to fight for rights and reject moral doubt

Some with thorns agree with abortion as the issue arises often
And the tiny life means little to those who want it eliminated
They think it is their life that is important and must be softened
So no one's life should be at anytime regulated or dominated

God's laws specifically denounce taking the life of another
So being able to choose an abortion is not spreading liberty
It gives one person a right but takes away one other's
And morals need to be questioned with this type of activity

Those who choose to follow God and have experienced this
Can obtain the Lord's pardon if truly sorry and not done again
He can see the heart and the mortal sin can be dismissed
So asking for forgiveness is the only way Heaven to gain then

Those with thorns must see they do not know their spiritual faults
It is because they never look into the soul to see what is wrong
Never realize that their spiritual shortcomings are assaults
That aid Satan to encourage and coax their weaknesses along

This condition is caused by a lack of humility
They believe in themselves and what they have accomplished
No thought of help that has been given or their human fallibility
And no fear that at the end of their days they may be banished

A change must be made and must come from the heart
Pride is a terrible thing and leads those with thorns from God away
The devil always takes advantage at this very part
And soon without knowing it they have truly lost their way

Then those who lose their way can inspire others with deceit
Some use public broadcasting to advertise a product or service
And with subliminal suggestions use sex and wealth to compete
This type of activity is not seen as a customer disservice

Basing needs on wants can promote subconscious thought
Spawning evil ideas such as adultery and pornographic desires
Ideas seen as valid and the need for gratification taken or bought
Needs that in the mind's eye must somehow be acquired

Is selling something or promoting an idea so important
That underlying ideas are needed to push the thought
This type of swaying people is planned carefully and constant
And unfortunately continues on until many people are caught

Swaying people can also be applied to the famous and known
What they contribute to the public and the contents that are found
Tells where their priorities are and if their love for God is shown
Or if worldly ways have rich and status oriented people bound

The ability they are given should be used for the good of all
To lighten peoples' hearts or provide respectable pleasure
If not used for good purposes the owner will back up to a wall
And the talent will be turned into a ruler for measure

So those with great talent need to watch and beware
That the gifts they were given are truly on loan
They were not given skills so their greatness they can declare
And continuously ensure their seed in bad soil is sown

But all souls must watch as they have some ability that was given
Skills allotted to use for the benefit of individuals they meet
These gifts should be used for another and the owner driven
To make peoples' lives happier and soothingly sweet

And always there are those who feel coveting is fine for the times
Wanting others' spouses and things are part of the way of life
Everyone does these things so they cannot possibly be a crime
Ignoring the fact that these actions cause heartache and strife

Why would they possibly want what others hold
Obtaining others' spouses or things will never gladness bring
Life will only turn into something boring and cold
And the same items that were taken become just another old thing

Instead of worrying about what their neighbors have or own
They need to look at their beings and change their lives inside
Adjusting not for material or physical things seen or known
But working towards spending eternity where Jesus does preside

So many ways and thoughts to lead them away from the Lord
And when the news of storms and despair and pestilence prevail
They look to Heaven and ask why they continue to be ignored
Sincerely questioning the floods and quakes and damaging hail

They truly are unaware that humans deserve what transpires
God sees what people ask Him for by what they do
And even innocent ones are affected not to hurt or destroy desires
But to change hearts and to help anyone touched a new life pursue

Amazingly those who have thorny soil and must live their own way
Seek God's aid when their path is paved with stumbling blocks
Those who must be free turn and may even to God pray
Until the path is clear and then they no longer are part of His flock

They should not be fooled at what the world tells them
Gradually those who want an immoral world will present more sin
And those who follow earthly ways will not object or condemn
But follow along blindly and with their lives allow the spin

They look at those around them but cannot see deep inside
Others' eyes obscure the image of God and mask the soul
It is not possible anymore as the feelings completely hide
The looks that could be read before are out of their control

God waits for them to enrich the soil and again let the seeds sprout
He loves always and will not let go until the final hour
They must listen for His call for He will not make them turn about
With their free will they must see He has eternal and final power

It is not too late to feed the seed that was given
He is waiting for a change of heart and a change of way
If they only ask for pardon they will be forgiven
Once they ask Him to be their Savior with Him they will stay

But they must grasp their current life and what they are now doing
They must see their sins and the gifts they are abusing
And see the activities and material things wanted they are pursuing
Then determine the true eternity they are currently choosing

Recall the prodigal son and how he demanded without a bow
He took his share and spent unwisely and really did not care
Then he became hungry and worked by the sweat of his brow
But by his hard work very little food or clothing did he bear

So he decided to go back to his father who lived well with much
He would go back to his father and work as a servant for his fate
But his father ran to greet him and with his arms his son did clutch
The son's robe and ring were returned and he was restored as great

God will do the same for those who change from their evil way
He waits with opened arms for the turn to finally take place
More will be given than was granted the prodigal son that day
God loves them and wants only in Paradise to see their lovely face

THE SEEDS THAT
FELL ON
FERTILE SOIL

Some seeds sowed by the Lord fell on soil that was fertile
These seeds are well fed as they accepted the Word
They work at understanding the Word and assume every hurdle
And continue to bear fruit and continue to be stirred

....

These are the people who welcome God in their lives and hearts
They gladly allow the Word to speak to them continuing to learn
They tell others about God and their love for Him impart
The Master is their way, truth, and life and to Him do they turn

Fertile soil Christians comprehend that they cannot go to the Father
They cannot achieve eternity in the Heavenly Home forever
Unless they know Jesus and do not consider Christianity a bother
A living relationship and privilege that they will never sever

These people are not perfect but they labor very hard
To learn and do God's will and always follow His call
To these God is their Savior and everlasting Guard
He is always with them through the good times and the squalls

They are the ones who try to bring joy to other lives by love
They adore God and love others as in their hearts He abides
Taking care of the sick and hungry as commanded by Above
Helping all come together as brothers and sisters and will not divide

These souls continue to nourish the wonderful seed
Through keeping their faith by accepting God's love and grace
And giving that love to others as a daily deed
Hoping others will turn to God and will someday see His face

Although these people still have their problems and inabilities
They understand they must continually work at their faults
Accepting the work mandatory to end failures and deficiencies
For they know they are God's people and the earth's delightful salt

They do not live by looking back with continuous regret
After confessing their sins and receiving absolution
Misdeeds they let go and unsuccessful times they try to forget
Learning from mistakes is the correct result and resolution

For God knows that everyone sins and has times of trouble
The tenacity of these people to serve their Master is what matters
Continuing to love their God and personal efforts they double
Each time Satan tries to grab them his hold they break and shatter

Others will know these servants as God's disciples
Because of the work accomplished and the future they see
Continuously spreading God's Word to all created peoples
To every person throughout society they will talk of He

Bad days they will try to ignore and continue to spread happiness
If failure occurs they will try again for their actions tell the story
Their focus is on living as God commands and alleviating sadness
This will guide others to Him and let them know God's glory

For only by giving will one truly receive
They know that God has given them everything they hold
And so great effort is applied to help others believe
By communicating their faith in God and ensuring history is told

The ones with fertile soil try to show humility in all they do
They have time for those they meet along the way
By listening and putting others first blessings they accrue
Their Christian ideals they apply and convey

Those who practice essential morality learn how awesome life is
They look around as they live each day and hear the quiet sounds
An understanding is gained that all creation is His
And they know that humility will ultimately bring them crowns

Endurance in doing the Almighty's wishes calms the souls
The perseverance dispels the troubles that come to them
They take the time to read and study the scrolls
Recognizing that all they have and all goodness from Him stems

Meekness is the way they bend to the God they exalt
They pass by the worldly things others crave
And turn their cheek to those who would assault
Concentrating on the spiritual world and not the physical grave

Their mildness is an offering to the only One who does matter
And they try to live each day in internal tranquility
Not living by wishing to impress others with chatter
But living with a spirit that believes in His eternal stability

Peace is what they choose to guide their thoughts
And praying in stillness causes the soothing silence to enrapture
Contemplating how their Lord died and for them bought
A blissful eternity this world can only spiritually capture

They are the sheep who know their God's voice
And as they kneel in prayer they remember the days
That as the sheep of old were killed for the Passover with rejoice
The Lord on the cross did speak His very last phrase

The Lord became the Sacrificial Lamb for all
And at His Passover the new covenant He did give
He asks all to accept this gift of love and to all He did call
A gift willingly given if for eternity they with Him will live

The Sacrificial Lamb who conquered forever death
Will be waiting as these souls drift from this earth at last
As these peoples' spirits are released with the final breath
The life lived will tell that Heaven they have gained and hold fast

They hold a healthy fear of God and what eternity can be
They fear the Lord but know to Him they are very precious
Mourning the mistakes they have made now they can see
The right way to live and for God to become infectious

This fear does not make them afraid or turn them away
The fear reminds them they have responsibility for their actions
Sorrow reminds them the laws given they must obey
That life must not for them cause meaningless distractions

This feeling is healthy and guides them to be strong
They know that they can depend on the support of Heaven
Effort is given to the vital things that need to be brought along
While knowing sins with sincere regret will always be forgiven

These are the people who look back over their past
And understand how God has been with them from the start
He was always with them and they never even asked
They went their merry way while He constantly did His part

Each stage of their lives they can see how He participated
And outcomes were changed miraculously without their aid
Unexpected events determined a new way of travel unanticipated
And the occurrence was always remembered and did not fade

They do not take credit for anything that they have accomplished
They know their life belongs to God and they were put on the path
Looking back at what was finished they have been astonished
And they see the work of God's great hand in the aftermath

They will not let pride tell them how skillful they are
They know that all that has been realized they were guided through
Someone invisible leads them not from afar
And they are seen as an individual not part of a vast queue

This showed them to trust in God above and know He is there
No matter what cross must be carried and throughout all life bear
Actions they must take to avoid the evil and nasty snares
Knowing for certain they and all others are in His care

Not peer pressure nor false superiority can sway their path
Justice is sought for all and towards God's commands
They know those who harm unjustly will feel the Holy Wrath
And true believers will work to stop injustice taking crucial stands

They will not follow the impulses of the current times
Allowing inward emotion to override the edicts God has given
Or think that man knows best and can commit moral crimes
But they will encourage those who falter to ask to be forgiven

For God is a jealous God and demands that all worship Him only
Adoring anything or anyone else will not bring lasting pleasure
As eventually those obeying their own wants will become lonely
And they will slowly lose forever the wonderful eternal Treasure

Recall the religious leaders as the Lord the earth did walk
They became jealous and afraid of the Lord and all that He did do
And so they planned His demise and to the people did talk
But they all did cower as the sky turned dark from blue

Those with well fed seeds believe mercy to all should be given
They want God to forgive them and they must comply
The love they feel in their hearts make them driven
To ask God to forgive others too as they pray glancing at the sky

Gentleness flows to others as the seed is enriched further
They welcome their neighbor in peace and friendship
Wishing to help them along and biblically nurture
Knowing from the beginning all were joined in kinship

Watchfulness is vital to them so they do not let evil taint the heart
The nasty one will never quit trying as long as there is a chance
So thought must be used to deny wickedness and be smart
And forgiveness and love will always enhance this correct stance

For mercy is taught by the price the Lord did pay
He came to save humanity knowing His creation was lost by sin
He came to earth to pay the price not with His creatures to stay
And for those who would accept spiritual peace, He did win

Those with fertile ground understand why life is granted
Just as the Lord was born to die as everyone's Deliverer
They have a purpose and will not let their devotion be recanted
And they work to turn those who do not know God into a believer

They all take different routes to work for God and others
They work and strive out loud and behind the scenes
As they toil away their attention turns to their sisters and brothers
Working long hours and many days past their very means

Praying to God is accomplished all throughout the day
And when they need added help they ask others for them to pray
It is the avenue that they know they can take to keep evil away
And after each prayer is said they know it will be okay

These are the pure of heart with good intentions for all
Prayers are sent up Above for all they know and meet
At times they ask the angels and Saints to help others not to fall
And pray continuously that all will bow before the Mighty Seat

They will labor to practice humility and live to serve
Their spirits they will protect to avoid being soiled by anything
They are meek and poor of spirit and by their King will preserve
They will stay away from whatever the evil one will bring

At the Last Supper the Lord told His company
That the Son of Man did not come to be served
He came to serve and offer His life as ransom for many
A fate He gladly accepted but in no way deserved

Those who follow Him will do the same
They will serve until the stairs to Heaven are to them shown
Thanking the Holy One that He came for them to claim
They will thank God as they meet others kneeling at the Throne

This is the type of sensitivity given to those
Who believe and are open to the grace that He allows
They trust that what they need will be sent and disclosed
And they will stay close to their God as they continue to bow

They also accept discernment from the Holy Spirit
Seeing not with their eyes but with the wisdom placed in the heart
They have faith with the guidance in them inherit
And they know that they must listen and do their part

I find it amazing how only the seed with fertile ground
Believes in the unseen and knows without a sound
That the world's Creator is near them always and abounds
And this group is so very glad their Lord they have found

Many times they will face circumstances they cannot change
These events may last a short time or through their earthly being
They never do these types of experiences try to exchange
For these occasions all have great and lasting meaning

The different challenges that come do not affect their trust
Being unable to change the here and now can make life hard
But keeping hope throughout all tests helps them to adjust
And placing trials in perspective prevents them from being scarred

Every challenge must be seen as an opportunity for learning
To improve the perspective of a valuable lifetime duration
To see that life is not about selfishness or for things yearning
But to understand that all is given to guide toward salvation

These are the people who enjoy going to Mass
And they know the attendants from Heaven gather about
They listen for the multitude of angels singing as they pass
And know the Saints are among them who in life did not doubt

The Church is always full no matter what the eye can see
And praising of the wonderful Lord is done constantly
They look to Jesus who came to set all free
And know that this is the only place love is given so abundantly

As the piece of bread is raised to Heaven above
A miracle takes place as the bread is truly changed
The Holy Spirit comes over the altar with God's love
And the bread to the Holy Body of the Lord is duly exchanged

As the priest pours the wine into the chalice
It is changed as the Spirit comes over the gifts to make them Holy
And no matter what the devil does to show his terrible malice
They know the cup of ordinary wine turns into Sacred Blood solely

Prayer they use often and know that it is powerful
They know that Jesus came not to abolish the law but to fulfill it
He gave them a model in the garden that showed He was masterful
That they should pray for others and ask that their sins He omit

When they start to lose their way they listen for guidance
Inside they know when it comes and that they should obey
They choose God's way and are confident of their reliance
Then on bended knee they thank Him while they humbly pray

So prayer is used to help them change their actions and attitudes
Prayer helps them keep in focus and do as the Master commands
On their own or in the pew they thank God with gratitude
Praying that He will help them love all here and in other lands

They realize that keeping the Commandments they must do
The greatest of the Commandments are to love God and others
Through peace can they lead brothers and sisters to change anew
By goodwill others will listen about the Lord and Him discover

Love is what Mighty God wants and what will lead to Paradise
Without love nothing the Lord expects can be understood
Those wanting to spend forever with God must evolve and sacrifice
They are peacemakers and know all done with love creates good

Those with fruitful seeds feel the comfort of their Lord
They know they are God's children and they listen and follow
Ensuring support of the Church they serve but never are bored
While knowing the cause of opposition will feel pain and sorrow

Conscious that they cannot make others believe
Their job is to be compassionate and let God shine through them
With the awareness that the Holy Spirit will guide others to receive
And after others grasp then avoiding hell and being condemned

Those with lush seed suffer persecution for God and then behave
By trusting in God and living faithfully in the here and now
Knowing He is above building mansions for all who will be saved
Who are eager to be taken there and for eternity only to Him vow

They thank God for understanding how they feel inside
They know that God is never indifferent even when people may be
He will always be with them and in their hearts always abide
And they will always worship and thankfully look to Him to see

He knows the abilities and limitations of all of their natures
He will assess them one day but He does not allow others to judge
For others do not know their hearts or the position of their juncture
And God does not use in consideration the concept of a grudge

Recall the singing friar who to the monastery went
His parents were appalled and looked at his actions with regret
After seeing the peaceful joy the friar had his parents their ear lent
Now his father a Church deacon is becoming as his God he has met

The young friar looks to Heaven with love as he sings
Knowing the miracle he has seen and was permitted to witness
Thanking God for His forgiveness and all the blessings He brings
Thanking the Lord that those he loves his God they do confess

Those with productive soil will help those so badly in need
Those who are mentally suffering in this phase of the age
When many cannot come to terms they are looking to be freed
Those with mental illness need relief from confusion and rage

Through this period of history more and more call for support
The ones who do not know how to cope or tell others how they feel
As the fast pace all around them makes it hard for them to sort
And few listen anymore to a cry for help or appeal

The rich seed will not always be successful or know each to seek
But they will always extend love to each of those they meet
Then each one they find they will make feel wanted and unique
And those who are touched will hopefully feel that they are wheat

They will use the fertile seed to spread God's Word
And in His ways feed those who are near as the dew
Talking to those they meet will continue until all have heard
And speaking His laws until all possible for Him they accrue

For there are some in this world who have not heard
The Good News has not been spread that far
Then once all have been told their hearts will be stirred
And they will rejoice at the news of the Bethlehem star

This is the greatest action they can take for their neighbor
To ensure they understand that all have a Savior
When those who belong to Him toil and labor
They are growing and changing by their very own behavior

They know the time is coming when they will make a choice
Not to offend God by denying Him for any earthly reason
No matter what happens they will claim God with a loud voice
To deny Him would mean eternal damnation and treason

Evil continues to build worldwide capturing more and more seed
The doomed will do anything to stop them from the good way
Evil hates the moral and will pull all they can down to the weeds
The wicked will deny God as the Savior and that will be their say

No matter who evil hurts or rich seed it causes to be lost
Once the river Jordan they have crossed and Jesus' hand is taken
It will be clear all is as it should be at no fertile seed cost
Evil will enlist pain and sorrow only to frighten and shaken

They know God will not allow lasting pain for having faith in Him
Eternity will be ecstasy and worth all allegedly given for an instant
Evil cannot take anything and once in Heaven nothing will be dim
All that have kept their faith will be there and evil will be distant

Remember the persecuted Saints past and follow their lead
They would not deny God no matter what they were put through
They knew that when taken to Heaven they would be freed
No longer would they feel pain or agony or hear the devil's view

One of these Saints was Job from the Old Testament book
The devil told God that Job would not continue to serve Him
If he lost his fortune and the nasty one Job's friends took
Serving God was only a crutch for Job and a hollow whim

God gave the evil one permission to tempt Job and try
The devil took his fortune, family, friends, and his health
Job never turned from God and through this time he only did sigh
Job endured and God returned his people, health, and wealth

So they are not afraid of the time when worldly life will end
There is nothing on this earth that will be missed once gone
Material things will vanish and will not their way to Heaven wend
Once on God's side in Paradise they will see the beautiful dawn

They are not afraid of sickness, mental anguish, or helplessness
They know all must carry their cross just as their Master did
Jesus will be waiting with all of His gentleness
And for those who take up His cross nothing will be hid

Those with fertile soil thank God for all that must be experienced
For He has done so very much and shed His blood for all
Through suffering and strife their faith will be evidenced
So they take what comes with thankful prayer until the final call

They remember that Jesus several times said "Peace be with you"
He told them not to let hearts be troubled or to be afraid
They think not of the physical but of the spiritual and life anew
He is with them always so they will not be dismayed

Shhh hear what those with unfertile soil do not stop to listen to
Those who belong to God are still and know that He is near
The One who the wind and sea obey and all that He does subdue
They listen carefully and thoughtfully and all becomes very clear

They will continue to look to God and not let the world bother
It seems most are for themselves and others pay the price
But those with fertile soil have concern for their sister and brother
And forgive seventy times seven not just once or twice

They believe in the invisible and know that they are near
And that each life is important and to God very dear
He will always guide and hold each hand so there is no fear
They will not stop offering the Word even when sensing a sneer

The world is changing rapidly and evil when it can does curse
They focus on eternity and do as much good as can be done here
And like the disciples they stay steadfast and on the pathway terse
Keeping God's eternity as first priority and to all endear

What a privilege those who have accepted their seed experience
For they have discovered that the world cannot satisfy
But oh God's love and ways make all the difference
And once found there will be nothing else that can gratify

WHERE ARE
THEY NOW

I think of those already living life for the One they adore
Others are floundering along the path of an unhappy existence
I know most follow a course they totally love or will totally abhor
They will persist in choosing serenity or avoid Heavenly essence

I notice the rose and how it grows so poised and so beautifully
The fragrance it emits more magnificent than any human made
Nature's work and created with many colors artfully
The Mother's bloom in bouquets that delightfully cascade

Ah life was made to be lovely as the rose
A life full of calmness and inward tranquility
A presence that cheers the world around it and diminishes woes
A beauty that takes the breath and garnishes around with humility

Those I contemplate have lived long and varied lives up until today
How many really understand all the marvels God has for them done
Most of these have managed to live in a fog and kept Him at bay
Never giving Him credit for the refreshing rain or the drying sun

My heart aches to see the many who will ultimately lose their souls
Forgetting that the Savior was born to sacrifice for all
The multitude not making eternal plans or setting everlasting goals
And living life by ignoring the Divine Baby born after the fatal fall

I know that the world changed forever the day God arrived
History was split evermore from the ancient to the new
From that moment a fresh way was set and a new covenant derived
The world changed completely with an entirely different hue

Those who so casually go on and push their God away
Do not meditate on how He loves each one so
That He calls each person by name and at their side does stay
Holding their hand until the end when He finally does let go

Do they not see His creativity and all the joy He sends
Like sitting on the back porch step after the final days glow
And hearing a symphony as the crickets' violins bend
An orchestra humans cannot match or even try to grow

I watch at dusk while the fireflies come together for a while
And do a beautiful dance that lights the evening sky
The design of the Almighty Originator outdoes any other style
A true miracle and blessing seen by every eye

As usual most humans take these gifts for granted
Not even noticing the beauty that is in front of them each day
Unnoticed are the worlds great and small that walk or are planted
What a pity true joys of life are missed along so many ways

But I know that most do miss so much more
And they have nothing to look forward to or plan to see the light
Believing that religion and praying will never touch their core
Making money and buying things seems to be so very right

Most do not understand how wonderful Heaven will be
And all who are privileged to go there will awesome wonders see
Letting go of this soiled world and gaining Paradise with glee
Only in that Holy Place above will they truly be set free

Instead of working hard to make a statement here
The goal is to serve well now and Bliss to eventually gain
The effort must change from this level to the Heavenly tier
Not to settle for things that pass away and to the visible world deign

The material things that have been collected through the years
I see grasped tightly as though they at the end must be taken along
The thought of leaving them forever brings a tear
The belief is that material things are what make people strong

But material things are only temporary and finally fade away
Physical things corrode and tear and become useless to the person
And material things have no mind and cannot love or play
People buy the things and admire until they break or worsen

Remember the rich man who asked if he could follow the Lord
Christ said, "First go and sell all that you have and give to the poor"
The rich man turned and walked away as he had much stored
He refused to give up his things and the fine clothes that he wore

This life is not to see how much each can personally obtain
This life is to improve spiritual being and grow within
It is not the time to become so very selfish and uselessly vain
But to see in depth of what is to be and Ecstasy to win

They do not realize that time spent in this world is a testing phase
It is a time for all to grow, change, and serve the Trinity
A time to take in the countless blessings granted and give praise
A period to understand the graces given and come near to Divinity

Yes I remember when I was one of those who attention did not pay
How worldly things were so important and the beauty pushed away
Too busy with silly things to stop and enjoy the different displays
A schedule to keep and daily demands from which I could not stray

Oh how many times I have wished that I could go back
And change so many actions and ways through which others I hurt
That is not possible and all make errors having times that are black
But now I know these things happen so people change and convert

A tragedy to witness those who believe they have no choice
That they must live by being told who to follow and what to do
They lose the essence of directing their life and value of their voice
The victim, the used, those in the dark who little grew

I know how peer pressure and others in life can influence
Telling those they come in contact with how life ought to be
That the wants of each are fine and do not make a difference
That each can do as they please and then all will agree

Eventually these same turn God into their own image
Justifying anything they do with "God will understand"
They cannot possibly know God and Him they only envisage
They try to define God with the life they have planned

How life has changed and all need to see the fast paced world today
Those who dislike pious living want complete elimination
It seems that all who want to live dutiful lives and God's way
Are the main ones these days who experience discrimination

Oftentimes they say that life is for the living
They underestimate life and believe it is only for this world
If they persist in continuing this belief and misgiving
Their dreadful eternity too soon will be unfurled

God's will does not change to what each individual person craves
He was very clear in His laws and what He expects
When God leads a certain way this would the people's lives save
They must trust in God's ways and the final effects

They should not be fooled and believe that He does not see
They are never alone and they always have spiritual company
From His sight they can never hide or unnoticeably flee
Life that is believed to belong to them is always in His custody

Look to the farmer whose harvests were always plenteous
His neighbor's crops were not as ample and that person's yield slid
The farmer said the weather permitted his crops to be bounteous
The farmer wanted the same kind of weather that God did

Of course part of the reason some choose to follow a wicked will
Is because they are afraid of all this world can bring
And as they do not believe the consequences evil does instill
They focus on earthly events that create fear and make hands wring

I remember this type of fear and how it can affect
Instead of humans taking control the worldly things rule people
As days pass by all that can go wrong is what they expect
And all that is concentrated on is that there will be a sequel

The fear that is generated consumes lives each day
And coping becomes difficult when functioning this way
Relief is sought however it can be found while combating dismay
It is the only course to be taken where they feel they have a say

Gazing back at those I knew and what they finally decided to do
I feel shame as I did not work as one of God's people to offer aid
I did not think of others and that serving would help even a few
No thought did I give of holding a hand to help them not feel afraid

I did not care what my peers and acquaintances felt inside and did
Through most of those things I comforted them not at all
As I watched deeper and deeper into despair they slid
And I could almost hear the master of this world call

As time went by I knew that all can change by asking the Creator
No matter what type of existence is experienced or lived in
The request will be answered by the Holy Vindicator
The response will help them to avoid any fear or any sin

For Jesus lived on earth and knows how they feel
He knows the pain when someone dies or walks away
When others turn their back or are mean how long it takes to heal
He experienced all the hurts people suffer along the way

So they can decide to live as His servant and His way
Or they can refuse the graces He offers and go a different route
One way offers Heaven's light and the other them to hell as its prey
So they must learn to sprout or experience eternal drought

The Great Sacrifice was accomplished with a loving heart
Who else loves so much that they would take on sins of others
And would die experiencing such agony as their offered part
While giving love and healing to their earthly sisters and brothers

Those who decide to be producers are much more joyous beings
Those who live for themselves find very little joy in living
Serving God here on earth leads to understanding life's meaning
Living for oneself rarely offers peace or happiness in giving

The presence here for most was not given for why it is used
Instead of employing this life to grow for the hereafter
Time is spent learning worldly things and becoming the accused
It must be seen that this life is a realization and growing chapter

They must watch at each stage in their life what they are doing
It must be established if they are following God's will or theirs
The actions taken and how it is done tells what they are pursuing
Are they attending to God's or to their own personal cares

This is their chance to stop and look around and be aware
Of the wide or narrow path they are on and choosing now
This is their time to think hard and to understand and beware
If they want to stay where they are or for Him avow

No matter what creature level all must bow
The beautiful angel thrown from Heaven knows this well
And those unaware are hunted now by fiends with a furrowed brow
As the master of the underworld waits happily to see all go to hell

All their lives they must pay close attention
And they will be judged on all that they knew
If they ask for forgiveness no sin will be mentioned
All they need do is believe and be true

Remember all down the road of Emmaus they sought
All must walk that road as those before did do
Focusing on being spiritually lean or quite taught
And hopefully come to the same conclusion the disciples drew

For when God calls they must be ready to respond
And be ready to walk away and leave the dead to bury the dead
The time is now with God to create a lasting bond
And nevermore look back and hopelessly dread

THE
BEAUTIFUL

I am tired and of all of those who have appeared in my mind
I know that some will turn to God and some will stay the same
Many through their lives have been selfish, some have been kind
Some have taken responsibility for actions and some have blamed

As I peer back over what I have learned and seen
I feel shame for many deeds but also gratitude for God's grace
I pray others will look over their lives in detail as if on a screen
And turn to God alone and against Satan firmly brace

Lucifer comes not with horns but tied to the mild and attractive
He tricks those who would befriend him or what he has sent
And makes those who cannot discern think he is supportive
While he leads them down a despicable road that is ruddy and bent

For all of those who will not fertilize the seed the Lord gave
The devil will take power and will become their controller
They will be hurled to hell with the dragon and will be his slave
For all eternity this will never change and he will not be a consoler

I know that a distinct type of seed exists within different ones
Unfortunately the unfertile type of seed is becoming frequent
Fewer and fewer are attending Mass and honoring the Son
Attending to their personal needs only is the new sequent

They are not trying to improve their relationship with Jesus
They only concentrate on what they believe they want now
They do not care about their behavior and act facetious
Not to God but to earthly things do they bow

I know that now is the time that I can finally see
And at last am realizing life is a path of choices on a great journey
An unbelievable expedition if I choose that way and focus on He
Where I decide to gaze I see blessings that are many

The passage offers many learning experiences and trials
In the past I did not realize what happened right away
Examination was accomplished and then change instead of denial
And I sought until I understood and saw the sunny ray

I have learned what a great gift life is but life to many means little
Some give no thought to the deeds done and precious spirits broken
Nor do the lives mean much of those damaged and turned brittle
Time spent for others is seen as a required and empty token

Now that I have fertilized my seed life takes on a different value
The words faith, hope, and love are important to my heart
Spoken with conviction and used as life's avenue
Words that guide my thoughts and used for my path to chart

How the fertile heart sees all things differently
God's creation is seen rather than the world of material things
The beauty of seeing mountains and feeling the breeze so gently
Listening to the great ocean and the eagles broad spanned wings

Knowing that beyond this earthly life and world
An eternity filled with contentment and joy of the heart
Is waiting and when this life is through will finally unfurl
And never again will spirits that rise and God ever part

I thank God above for helping me along each step
As I peer back over time I know He has always been at my side
He has been there no matter if I tried or if I did misstep
God has always helped me up and each of my tears dried

Not everything worked out as I would have wanted
And there were things I asked for I never did receive
But I know He was there and at the right path pointed
And continued to help me until finally I did perceive

I pray that God will allow me into his Heavenly home
Where I can live with the love of my life forever
A place where I will never be alone or worriedly roam
Where fear or sadness I will feel again never

I pray for each and every one and hope dear God they will heed
I hope that they will turn to the Savior and for others pray
That Satan they will turn their backs and ignore his terrible pleads
And on the day they face their Lord they are not turned away

Oh look closely and all can surely see Who stands in sight
Those about Him with the beauty of their aura shining very bright
There is no fear or sorrow that makes me want to take flight
The clock ticks; time will end before the close of this very night

The shining light comes nearer and nearer
The air is full of calm and tenderness and peace
I have no more inabilities and all things come clearer and clearer
The earthly world no longer matters as it disappears and does cease

THE TEN COMMANDMENTS

I. I am the Lord your God, who brought you out of the land of Egypt, out of the house of bondage. You shall have no other gods before Me. You shall not make for yourself a graven image, or any likeness of anything that is in heaven above, or that is in the earth beneath, or that is in the water under the earth. You shall not bow down to them or serve them.

II. You shall not take the name of the Lord thy God in vain.

III. Remember the Sabbath day, to keep it holy.

IV. Honor your father and your mother.

V. You shall not kill.

VI. You shall not commit adultery.

VII. You shall not steal.

VIII. You shall not bear false witness against your neighbor.

IX. You shall not covet your neighbor's wife.

X. You shall not covet your neighbor's house, nor his field, nor his servant, nor his handmaid, nor his ox, nor his ass, nor anything that is your neighbor's.[2]

COMMANDMENT I

I am the Lord your God, who brought you out of the land of Egypt, out of the house of bondage. You shall have no other gods before Me. You shall not make for yourself a graven image, or any likeness of anything that is in Heaven above, or that is in the earth beneath, or that is in the water under the earth. You shall not bow down to them or serve them.

This Commandment requires that people:

Love God above everything and all creatures for Him and because of Him. Believe in Him and hope in Him with all their heart, soul, and strength.

Nourish and protect their faith with prudence and vigilance and reject everything that is opposed to it.

Practice adoration.

Pray

Sacrifice

Ensure fidelity to promises made to God (promises of baptism, marriage, etc.).

Worship genuinely both individually and socially.

Respectfully venerate icons portraying a person such as Mary the mother of Jesus, angels, and Saints who lead us to God incarnate. This does not include worshiping or adoration of the images as that is for God alone.

This Commandment forbids things such as:

Idolatry

The worship of false gods and goddesses

Polytheism

Worship of the devil

COMMANDMENT I continued

This Commandment forbids things such as:

Worship of the stars, sun, or moon as in astrology

Making golden calves

Building temples to Isis

Worshipping statues of Caesar

Voluntary doubt

Incredulity

Heresy

Apostasy

Schism

Indifference

Ingratitude

Luke warmness

Spiritual sloth

Hatred of God because of pride

Superstition

Divination

Magic or sorcery

Tempting God

Sacrilege

Simony

Atheism

Agnosticism

Despair

COMMANDMENT II

You shall not take the name of the Lord thy God in vain.

This Commandment requires that people:

Honor the name of God.

Witness to the Lord's name by confessing the faith without giving way to fear.

Preach and catechize permeated with adoration and respect for the name of our Lord Jesus Christ.

Respect promises made in God's name.

Remember God calls each person by name, so the name of each person must be respected.

Begin prayers with the Sign of the Cross: in the name of the Father, the Son, and the Holy Spirit.

This Commandment forbids the following:

Do not abuse God's name or introduce God's name into speech except to bless, praise, and glorify it.

Do not utter against God in hatred, reproach, or defiance which is blasphemy. This includes language against Christ's Church, Jesus's mother Mary, Saints, sacred things.

Do not use God's name to cover up criminal practices.

Do not use God's name to reduce people to servitude.

Do not use God's name to torture people or put them to death.

Do not use God's name for false oaths.

Perjury

COMMANDMENT III

Remember the Sabbath day, to keep it holy

The seventh day is a Sabbath of solemn rest holy to the Lord.

The Sabbath day recalls creation.

The Sabbath recalls Israel's liberation from bondage in Egypt.

God entrusted the Sabbath to Israel to keep as a sign of the irrevocable covenant.

The Sabbath is for the Lord, holy and set apart for the praise of God, His creation, and His saving action on behalf of Israel.

God rested and was refreshed on the seventh day and man ought to rest and let others, especially the poor, be refreshed.

The Sabbath was made for man, not man for the Sabbath. The day should be used for doing good, for saving life rather than killing.

Sunday is expressly distinguished from the Sabbath which it follows chronologically every week; for Christians its ceremonial observance replaces that of the Sabbath. In Christ's Passover, Sunday fulfills the spiritual truth of the Jewish Sabbath and announces man's eternal rest in God.

On Sundays and other holy days of obligation the faithful are bound to participate in the Mass.

COMMANDMENT IV

Honor your father and your mother.

Children must obey their parents.

Grown children must respect their parents and see to the care of their parents when they become old and infirm.

Children owe their parents respect, gratitude, just obedience, and assistance.

Parents have the first responsibility for the education of their children in the faith, prayer, and all the virtues. They have the duty to provide as far as possible for the physical and spiritual needs of their children.

Parents should respect and encourage their children's vocations. They should remember and teach that the first calling of the Christian is to follow Jesus.

This Commandment includes and presupposes the duties of parents, instructors, teachers, leaders, magistrates, those who govern, all who exercise authority over others or over a community of persons.

COMMANDMENT V

You shall not kill.

A better translation from the original Hebrew is murder.
Killing an innocent person is murder. Killing to save your own
life against someone who is an aggressor is not murder and not
immoral.

God alone is the Lord of life from its beginning until its end: no
one can under any circumstance claim for himself the right
directly to destroy an innocent human being.

Jesus added to the fifth Commandment the banning of anger,
hatred, and vengeance.

Forbids doing anything with the intention of *indirectly* bringing
about a person's death.

Human life must be respected and protected absolutely from the
moment of conception.

Direct euthanasia consists in putting an end to the lives of
handicapped, sick, or dying persons. It is morally unacceptable.

Suicide is contrary to love for the living God.

We must take reasonable care of life and physical health entrusted
to us by God.

Scandal is a grave offense when by deed or omission it
deliberately leads others to sin gravely.

Because of the evils and injustices of war, we must do everything
reasonably possible to avoid it.

COMMANDMENT VI

You shall not commit adultery.

This Commandment forbids the actual physical acts of immoral sexual activity of the following:

Adultery

Fornication

Prostitution

Pornography

Homosexual activity

Masturbation

Rape

Group sex

Pedophilia

Incest

Bestiality

Necrophilia

COMMANDMENT VII

You shall not steal.

This Commandment forbids taking someone else's property.

Cheating people of their money or property.

Depriving people of their just wage.

Not giving an employer a full day's work for a full day's pay.

Embezzlement

Tax evasion

Fraud

Vandalism

Those responsible for business enterprises are responsible to society for the economic and ecological effects of their operations.

Access to employment and to professions must be open to all without unjust discrimination: men and women, healthy and disabled, natives and immigrants.

Not to enable the poor to share in our goods is to steal from them and deprive them of life.

It is unworthy to spend money on animals that should as a priority go to the relief of human misery. One can love animals; one should not direct to them the affection due only to persons.

COMMANDMENT VIII

You shall not bear false witness against your neighbor.

Lying

Intentionally deceiving another by speaking a falsehood.

Duplicity, dissimulation, and hypocrisy.

Equivocation concerning the faith.

Perjury

Rash judgement.

Respect for the reputation and honor of persons forbids all detraction and calumny in word or attitude.

Flattery, adulation, or complaisance encouraging and confirming another in malicious acts and perverse conduct.

Revealing the truth to someone who does not have the right to know it.

Users should practice moderation and discipline in their approach to the mass media.

Journalists have an obligation to serve the truth and not offend against charity in disseminating information.

Professional secrets must be kept. Confidences prejudicial to another are not to be divulged.

COMMANDMENT IX

You shall not covet your neighbor's wife.

This Commandment forbids intentional desire and longing for immoral sex.

Every one who looks at a woman lustfully has already committed adultery with her in his heart.

COMMANDMENT X

You shall not covet your neighbor's house, nor his field, nor his servant, nor his handmaid, nor his ox, nor his ass, nor anything that is your neighbor's.

This Commandment forbids:

The wanting or taking of someone else's property.

Theft

Envy which is sadness at the sight of another's goods and the immoderate desire to have them for oneself.

Feeling of greed of what others have.

Feeling of jealousy of what others have.

Greed and the desire to amass earthly goods without limit.

Avarice arising from a passion for riches and their attendant power.

The desire to commit injustice by harming our neighbor in his temporal goods.

THE
BEATITUDES

Blessed are the poor in spirit,
for theirs is the kingdom of heaven.

Be humble, be detached from material things.

Blessed are they who mourn,
for they shall be comforted.

Mourn for your sins and others sins.

Blessed are the meek,
for they shall inherit the earth.

Be meek and gentle as a dove.

Blessed are they who hunger and thirst for
righteousness, for they shall be satisfied.

Hunger and thirst for Christ.

Blessed are the merciful,
for they shall obtain mercy.

Show mercy to others.

Blessed are the pure in heart,
for they shall see God.

Be pure of heart and see with the heart.

Blessed are the peacemakers,
for they shall be called sons of God.

Be of goodwill and submit to God.

Blessed are they who are persecuted for
righteousness' sake, for theirs is
the kingdom of Heaven.

Keep faith in God whatever comes.

Blessed are you when men revile you and
persecute you and utter all kinds of evil against
you falsely on My account. Rejoice and be glad,
for your reward is great in Heaven.

Thus they persecuted the prophets
who were before you.[2]

REFERENCES

1. *Padre Pio, The True Story*, Ruffin, 1991
2. *Catechism of the Catholic Church*, Second Edition, 1997